Daddy, this is it.
Being-with My Dying Dad

ISBN: 0-9919-2070-8
ISBN-13: 9780991920709

Daddy, this is it.
Being-with My Dying Dad

Julie Saeger Nierenberg

Thank you in advance for reading this book.
Please be kind to review it on Amazon.
Your reviews will assist me with future projects.

Farewell, Dear Father

The light beings are gathered now
In that place beyond dimension
That place we cannot know, but know awaits
Gathered they are to receive you at journey's end
Welcoming you now, in the ecstasy of death
Bathing you in the pure light of absolute peace
Blessing you with the comfort of release from
  all burdens

Farewell, dear father, farewell
Those whom you've left now grieve at our loss
Yet know that our hearts are cleansed by those
  salty tears
And we will go on loving
Sustained indeed by the love of God
So faithfully expressed by you

Farewell, dear father, farewell
Though you have passed into the light beyond
The eternal light that shined through you
Will never be forgotten
Peace be with us, as it is with you
May we too know the eternal comfort
Of resting in the arms of God
Farewell, dear father, farewell

By Louis C. Saeger, April 28, 2012

Prologue

Today I felt a strong response to a "Tough Love" email from blogger Craig Ballantyne of *Early to Rise* fame. To paraphrase his powerful message, "When we refrain from doing our best, and from succeeding at our goals, we hurt others." For some of us, there is a selfish reason why we hold back:

We protect ourselves from the criticism of others.

When we delay the actions we need to take to succeed, because of perfectionism or procrastination, we may not realize the consequences of our doing so. By postponing, or failing altogether to complete our project, we withhold its potential benefit from others. Craig's message really spoke to me. In fact, it *yelled* and motivated me to resume-to-completion this project.

A few days ago, a friend called our home to confirm that he received our recent voicemails. He delayed answering, he explained, because he'd been holding his dad's hand, being at his side, as his father prepares to die. Our friend said,

> "Birth is such a joyful and beautiful process.
> It's a real shame that death can't be like that.
> Or at least, it's not like that for my dad, for us."

But it can be, I thought. As his painful words echoed in my heart and head, I felt unprepared to voice my feelings about the experience of death. Though I am not living within the same paradigm that our friend and his dad share, I do believe that death *can be* a beautiful event, and that a life can be celebrated with joy at its end in a way that honors and nurtures the dying and the bereaved.

A third message came to me a few days prior to these calls-to-action. My tale may seem rather silly to some readers, and that's okay with me, as silly is a divine gift just like any other perspective. Try to imagine the way it happened for me.

While riding on a streetcar, my gaze drifted to the wall under the window where a sign jumped out at me:

KEEP ARMIN

Keep Armin? That's my dad's name—Armin. *He's messaging me from the Great Beyond!* Could my dad be reminding me to keep him front and center, to keep the promise that I made to him to write his story, our story, and share it with you? I took this message to heart, feeling its nudge, and I eventually got the *Aha* to KEEP [my] ARM IN when sitting near the streetcar window. It took me a minute or two to get that second meaning.

Now I invite you to enjoy our story and celebrate the worthiness of its telling.

1

I miss you, Daddy.

Daddy, I promised you I would continue the story, your story and our story, after you could no longer write. Today is the day I start.

In those moments between your last breath and my realization that it was, I felt many things—pain, sorrow, relief, surprise, wonder—all imbued with so much gratitude and peace that your struggle to live and to die at the same time was over.

It's been three weeks, and I handled them pretty well for the most part, until yesterday. That's when I melted down. That's when it truly hit me that I will never know another love like yours, another bond like ours, another unconditional space where I grow and flourish without demands or expectations, with boundless acceptance, unceasing encouragement and a shared history that goes all the way back to my first breaths.

You are my Daddy, and there will never be another like you. I miss you.

2

1100 More Days

For the past three years, since his diagnosis with cancer, I talked to my father daily—with few exceptions. When there were exceptions I felt the pull, the desire to check in. It was not so much for him that I did it. The daily conversations were for me. I wanted to be as close as I could be. With him living in Tulsa and me in Toronto most of the time, that was how I nurtured the connection.

Each phone call was important to me, a source of equilibrium and completion in my daily life. Sometimes I told him details about my day, about my life partner Earl, about my daughters' teenage milestones or about the weather; and mostly I just listened to what Dad wanted to share with me.

He rattled off little facts about his day: the pre-breakfast stroll in the hallway of his retirement center, the weight gain or loss he so closely followed, his meal and snack choices, the distance he traveled with his 'Hill o' Beans' walking buddies, the savoring of his French vanilla cappuccino, the encouraging news from his cancer doctor, the discouraging news from his eye specialist, the writing progress on his most recent memoir, the latest ideas for the next juicy story, the cherished rendezvous with an old friend, the challenges of his worsening eyesight, the unplanned nap in his rocker recliner, the dinner he shared with my stepmom Lucy at a favorite restaurant, her own health concerns and struggles, the copies of his book signed and sold, the recent conversations or visits with my other three siblings or with their children, and so on.

My dad told me everything he could think of to share about his day, and sometimes he told me twice. He wanted to stay on the phone with me and be together with me any way he could. So we were together in our talking and our listening and in the pauses between the words, making time for our hearts to be united. We knew our time together was coming to an end, and although we didn't know when that would happen, we knew it was inevitable and coming sooner than we wished.

My father was fortuitously diagnosed with cancer after an acutely blocked ilium landed him in the hospital—fortuitous because, without the blockage happening when it did, his metastatic tumor would have spread further and faster. We would have had less time with him. And the sudden blockage didn't occur simply because of the bowel cancer's growth; it was precipitated by his worsening blindness.

For years Dad had advanced and ever-worsening glaucoma, untreatable with available medications due to his allergic reactions. In his last few years he also had the kind of macular degeneration that did not respond to treatment. Surgeries for the glaucoma and cataracts, visits to specialists for the latest developments in eye disease treatments, new glasses after new glasses after new glasses. . . All were tried and failed to ease the progressing blindness.

Dad did whatever was in his power to continue to see as well as he could. He faithfully applied thrice-daily eye drops, performed a ritual of eye exercises and took a very costly regimen of supplements, the latest and greatest to preserve eyesight. He gulped a handful of these 'magic vision restoration pills'—along with his few prescribed medications—morning, noon and night.

And one day, because of my dad's poor eyesight, he also ingested a larger-than-capsule-sized supplement package desiccator labeled *Do Not Ingest*. When the surgeons removed that little cylinder from the blockage between the small and large intestines, they credited it with prolonging his life. Without that foreign object lodging in the constricted area that the tumor created, the cancer would have grown much larger and spread much further before being detected and killed him years earlier than it finally did. Instead, he lived to enjoy so many more rich days of life, over a thousand of them.

When I tell that story, I get goose bumps.

3

Sooner or Later

Despite the 'luck' of the occlusion and subsequent removal of his tumor, Dad harbored the beginnings of malignancy. It first spread to his liver, and the doctor removed almost half of that organ in a big surgery that beat him down emotionally and energetically. But he soon rallied by setting incremental goals, physical goals that also assisted his mental and emotional progress. Dad announced and then systematically beat each goal. "By next Monday I want to. . ." And by the previous Friday, he was already doing it. I cheered him on and listened to his doubts about having the ability and the will to come back again at his age.

He repeated this goal-achievement pattern with each next phase of cancer growth and cancer treatment. And as he lived with malignant cancer's incremental spread, we all learned so much about new developments in treatment regimens and new ways to target and *zap* a tumor without wiping out the human body where it grew.

Dad couldn't tolerate traditional chemotherapy. When he tried it, his remaining eyesight worsened significantly. He was not willing to trade that precious vision for the dubious benefits of the six-month chemo regimen. Instead he agreed to other creative options of treatment.

These choices worked effectively right up until they didn't, right up until his most recent hospitalization when the attending physician clumsily announced that we should visit with the hospice coordinator and get that support system set up before Dad was discharged from the hospital with no further treatment options.

Hospice?

How could that be? Why, he just received encouraging news from the oncologist days before! Yes, he knew he had an upper respiratory bug and was in the hospital to regain his strength before going back to his independent living apartment.

Did the doctor say "hospice"?

The physicians disgracefully bumbled this stage of Dad's care, and such an important phase: communication of the bad news, the *worst* news, the 'there is nothing we can do now' end-of-life news.

The oncologist who visited Dad's bedside the day before presumably didn't want to explain that the latest tests confirmed more tumors growing in his liver, abdomen and lung. This day's doctor thought the previous one had surely explained the extent of the spread, because notes in Dad's chart indicated the oncologist knew the findings. Together this 'tag team' of physicians traumatized Dad unnecessarily with the abrupt and backhanded delivery of this life-changing news.

I thank the Universe that I was there with Dad to 'translate' the newest radiological findings and to reassure,

8

comfort and confirm, to ease the unexpected blow—even if just a little bit—by absorbing it along with him.

There wasn't much I could do to prevent the emotional backdraft that visibly stunned the news-bearing hospitalist as the realization washed over him: he had 'blown it' by assuming Dad and I already knew what prompted him to suggest our meeting with hospice staff. I felt a bit sorry for the doctor, but mostly I was angry at the way this news was delivered, no matter who was at fault in the end.

"*Hospice?* No more treatments? No more goal setting and no more. . . no more. . . everything. *This is it* then. Life is coming to an end and I'm not ready. I have more life to live. There's more life in me. I'm not ready for this news. *Hold me,* Julie, *hold me!*" my father reached for me through these broken words.

And then the tears came. I held him as well as I could in the hospital bed. We cried and cried.

"I'm so glad you are here. Thank you for being here, Julie."

"I'm glad to be here, Daddy. I'm glad I am here. This is where I want to be, Daddy." Even at 86 years of age, I called him 'Daddy' (and I always will).

We cried some more. And then we talked it over again, everything the doctor had shared and what that meant for Dad's future days, for *our* future as his family.

Then, one by one, Dad and I contacted my stepmom and each of my three siblings with the news of his imminent release from the hospital and his transition into long-term nursing care and hospice. We called his closest friends. I emailed the cousins and many other friends.

Again and again we repeated the story: *Dad will not return to his apartment. He will not be getting better this time. He will be on hospice and facing the end of life. Sorry to have to convey this news. Thank you for your caring support.*

4

Beginning to Accept

But my father didn't feel like dying. He felt full of life and longing to live. He had more to do, more to say, more to feel, to taste, to write, to experience. He wasn't ready to die. He was angry and sad, disappointed and confused, accepting and unaccepting, and more than a little bit agitated. He was scared.

The next morning my sister Laura joined us at the hospital and we met with the hospice coordinator. Dad listened to the explanation of services that hospice would provide, asking questions when he wanted clarification, listening as we daughters also asked for more details. At the same time, we had a telephone connection with my stepmom, rehabilitating in another facility, so that Lucy could hear the same information we heard and receive answers to any of her questions.

They gave us explanatory pamphlets and brochures, and eventually a hefty notebook of information, about the benefits and protocols of hospice care.

It was up to Dad whether to accept hospice services. Doing so meant giving up any plans for pursuing further cancer treatment. Once placed on hospice, he was agreeing to the protocol of end-of-life care. These were the rules and regulations established by Medicare.

He could *opt out* of hospice at any time, an amusing thought.

We discussed our limited choices and agreed to the extra layers of hospice care to be provided onsite in the skilled nursing wing at Dad and Lucy's retirement center. Hospice's services included end-of-life specialty training of all their staff, attentive RN-level nursing, 'extra' bathing, 24-hour telephone triage access to support, social worker visits, wheelchair, oxygen, practical day-to-day supplies, medications, morphine (for when the time comes), as well as follow-up services for survivors of the deceased.

We were thankful these things were offered and took advantage of them.

5

Comforting Surroundings

The following day we moved Dad to his room in the skilled nursing section of his retirement center, doing our best to reassure him about his surroundings. With his limited vision, that wasn't always easy.

"Where is my clock with the big hands?" He needed that clock to note the time and anticipate his medication doses, naps, phone calls to his wife Lucy (currently in the rehab facility across town), etc.

We brought the clock from his apartment and installed it across from his bed on the wall.

We brought his prayer shawl, lovingly crocheted with prayer-infused stitches by his Quaker friend.

We brought Teddy, his beloved stuffed bear that his wife Lucy gave him as a special gift to his Inner Child.

We brought some copies of his book of memoirs, *Sowing My Quaker Oats*, to share with visitors.

We brought his favorite rocker recliner so he could sit there if he wanted, or we could sit there and be with him.

We brought his radio and CD player so he could hear music. Laura brought him a CD recording of Dad's mother's voice singing beautifully and of Dad's father's voice telling a tale of his youthful visit to the St. Louis World's Fair.

We brought the little cardinal called Bandit, a stuffed toy that my daughter Valerie gave him during his first hospitalization for cancer. "Bandit watches over me every day," Dad told us. "And sometimes he steals from the rich to give to the poor," he added with a silly grin.

We children, stepchildren, grandchildren and some great-grandchildren came to visit Dad. My brother Bob and sister Laura came from our hometown, 75 miles away. My brother Lou came from Minnesota. Our stepsiblings came from across the state and across the country. My daughters came from across town. My nieces and nephews came from near and far as well.

All wanted to be with Dad while a visit was still possible. He was so glad to be together with each of us.

Friends and colleagues came too, and he enjoyed their many visits.

When I returned to Toronto, he looked so good, sounded so strong, hugged me close and thanked me for our time together.

Oh, dear God, it was so hard to leave. We didn't know how long he'd be with us, but the initiation of hospice services meant the doctor estimated six months or less. I bought my plane ticket to return shortly after Dad would turn 87 in April.

6

A Spurt of Recovery

Back home I dove into my freelance work routine and called Dad every day, sometimes twice. Within the next ten days, he told me that he was working to get out of bed by himself, then walking with his walker, then setting a goal to see his walking buddies in the retirement center's bistro where he planned to share a cappuccino.

And he did just that.

Dad went out 'the escape hatch'—his name for the nursing section's double doors—walked through the halls, leaning on his walker and adorned in his bathrobe, and met his friends for coffee and the latest retirement center 'gossip.' That's what he called the news they shared about themselves, their families and the other retirement center 'inmates,' their humorous self-reference.

"Hip, hip, hooray, Dad! You did it!" I cheered him on as I always had. *You reached your goal*, I thought. *Still full of life*, I thought. "How was that cappuccino? How are your Hill o' Beans buddies?"

"Good, great, all good!" came his answer along with all the details he could remember. Several in the group had asked about me. I walked with the Hill o' Beans gang when I was in Tulsa visiting Dad, and had for several years. I shared their stories and the coffee time after the walk through the halls. I followed their ups and downs, their losses of dear friends and spouses, their hospitalizations and recoveries, their family visits and other joys.

I was so glad he made it to this goal, to be with them on that Monday morning, sipping cappuccino, *ahhh*. . .

It was Dad's last time to share such a meeting with friends.

7

Noticeable Decline

That same week Dad started going downhill, his strength ebbing, his ability to walk lessening noticeably and now reserved for a daily visit to his beloved Lucy, whose new location was in a room right next door to his. She couldn't get out of bed yet, but he could do so with assistance. Each morning he mustered all his strength to share his limited time at her bedside, cheering her on as she began physical therapy, rubbing her feet or her head, lovingly being present as only he could.

Day by day over the next two weeks, the nature of our telephone conversations changed dramatically. The calls were now a strain. Dad was running out of energy, things to say and any milestones to share.

He was running out of time.

Our roles reversed and I became the one wanting to linger for one more sentence, one more glimpse into his day and one more conveyance across the miles of our concern and affection.

"Thank you, Earl and Julie. Thank you for calling," came almost immediately after Dad answered his phone. "I love you both. Goodbye now."

Multiple times a day I checked with my sister Laura via email and phone to see if she was getting the same lack of news and precipitous drop in his level of engagement. She was.

Should I come now versus waiting the two more weeks?

She didn't know what to advise. She'd ask the hospice nurse. Dad rallied before, as we knew, time and again.

Each day I called at agreed-upon optimal times to catch him awake and alert. He was glad that I called, expressed his love and sometimes briefly related frustrations with unresponsive care or his growing confusion.

He couldn't see the clock on the wall anymore.

He didn't want to listen to music.

He didn't want friends to visit.

He didn't want to eat much.

He wanted to say goodbye now.

"I love you, Daddy. Bye for now. I'm coming soon. I'll be with you soon."

Once when I called, I reached him in a midday panic.

"Julie, *oh Julie*, I called for the nurses' aides. I pushed my button several minutes ago. And they aren't coming. *No one is coming!*"

18

"What's happening, Daddy? Can you tell me exactly what's wrong?"

"I was visiting with Lucy next door and barely walked back here with my walker. Then I almost collapsed. I am too exhausted to lift my legs into the bed. I'm going to fall if they don't come soon. I'm afraid *I will fall!*"

"Daddy, are you sitting on the seat of the walker? Or are you sitting on the edge of the bed?"

"The bed. I'm on the edge of the bed. And I can't sit up any longer. I will fall soon!"

"Daddy, can you hold onto the walker and let go of your position enough to gently roll to the side, to let your body relax onto the bed so that you don't fall off the bed?"

"No, I can't do that because I can't lift up my legs. I will hurt myself. It won't work and I'm so scared I will fall any minute. I can't—oh, *here they are!* Someone is here. Okay! Help me, *please*, Miss! I am falling!"

Click! Understandably, I was cut off with no goodbye this time.

Later, I called to confirm all was resolved, but Dad was understandably shaken by this episode. That was the last time he walked to visit with Lucy next door, the last time he walked with his walker on his own, though it was a couple of days later when I realized that.

8

A Light Dream

Monday arrived and it was nearly 5:00PM in Toronto. I still had work to do on my current project deadline and wanted to shut my eyes for a few minutes and come back to it refreshed. And so I reclined on the couch, just breathing and being still.

Within minutes I drifted between waking and sleeping, not caring about the distinction, and an amazing thing happened.

My head was filled with a bright light. Out of the light emerged two smaller ones, the one I perceived as 'I' and the other—most assuredly—as my dad.

We romped and played, danced and embraced, shared our two 'lightbodies' as one for just an instant, and I was filled with joy, lightness, happiness and comfort.

I woke up smiling at just a few minutes past 5:00, refreshed and ready to work.

Hmmm, *that was weird.*

Later, the same day when I called my dad at our agreed-upon time after supper, he chastised me, saying, "Why did you wake me up at 4:00, Julie, when you know that is when I am napping?"

Huh?

"What did you say, Daddy?"

Did I hear him correctly?

"Today you woke me up at 4:00, and that is when I always nap, you know. So I'm just reminding you."

What in the world? Okay, maybe not in *this* world.

4:00 his time was 5:00 in my zone.

Though I clearly knew that I hadn't telephoned him during his nap, I didn't contradict Dad, as any confusion about points of remembered fact caused him anxiety and agitated him at this point in his journey. Instead, I confirmed our agreement not to call except at the two best times we had set.

I wondered if he also experienced our 'Lightbody Soul Dance,' or whatever it was. I didn't bring it up to him.

9

Time to Be-with

On Friday morning, a week before my scheduled trip to Tulsa, I received a call from my sister Laura, saying that the hospice nurse had visited twice in two days and was currently consulting with our brother Lou—an anesthesiologist who specializes in pain management—about Dad's pain. Lou had arrived in Tulsa the night before.

Dad's breathing and heart rate slowed considerably and other signs indicated he was slipping.

Hospice enlisted 'round-the-clock aides to assist with any immediate needs he might have. This service was provided in what they estimated would be the final 48-72 hours of life.

Then Laura told me, in the nurse's opinion, it would be good for me to come right away if I wanted to be with Dad in his final days.

Oh, my! This was the news I didn't want to hear, but I was thankful there might be time enough to get there.

I spent that Friday scrambling to get flights from Toronto to Tulsa just as quickly as possible and ended up with two connections versus the single stopover I usually make, and I could live with that.

By Saturday evening I arrived in Tulsa.

Lou and Laura met me at the airport, and, as we drove to the retirement village, they brought me 'up to speed' on Dad's condition. It wasn't good.

Earlier in the day he yelled at an aide—way out of character for Dad, and he also refused food and drink. His vital signs were slipping and he turned down a medication offered to ease his increasing pain, saying he didn't want to feel the way that medicine made him feel.

It was late when we got to his room, so we said a brief hello and goodnight, wishing him a good sleep. Goodbye till morning.

10

Love Has Eternal Life

Sunday morning I arrived at the retirement center as early as I could. Dad rallied a bit and ate a good breakfast. He was glad to see me (and also the cappuccino I had purchased moments before).

I was delighted to see his improved mood, alertness and desire to converse. We chatted about Earl and my daughters, Kerry and Valerie. We talked about how Dad was feeling and about his beloved Lucy in the room next door.

And then in a private moment, he hugged me close and assured me, "My love will never die, Julie. God's love for you is also eternal. *God is love* and that love never dies."

"Thank you, Daddy. I believe what you say is true. Thank you for saying it."

"Now, are you ready to release me? Are you and I finished?"

A little confused over that, I hesitated to answer, so he rephrased and asked, "Are you finished with me?"

"Well, I don't want to say 'yes' to that, Daddy. Are you finished with me?" I asked.

"Are you ready to take responsibility and answer my question?" he asked, as kindly as he could.

With tears in my eyes, I looked right into his and said, bravely, "I am complete with you, Dad. I have nothing pending with you, nothing that we haven't cleared up or handled. Our relationship is as close and loving as it could be, and I am complete. Am I finished with you? All right, I will take responsibility and say, 'Yes, I am finished when you are finished. When you are ready to go, I am okay with that, Dad.' Okay?"

"Okay. Thank you, Julie. You are my one and only Julie, and I love you so much. I have always loved you and always will. You are so special to me, and our love is eternal. Anytime you want to feel my love, anytime you want to feel God's love, you just need to ask. Ask for it, and it is there for you, always there, and always will be."

"Daddy, I believe that you will always be with me and I with you. My heart and your heart are one. Thank you for your endless love. Thank you for being the very best Dad I could ever have or ever want to have. You are the perfect dad."

"Oh, I believe I made my share of mistakes, Julie. Lots of mistakes."

"Yes, Daddy. And I thank you for those too. It is through those mistakes that we learn how to go forward and make choices, necessary choices, and how to heal and to forgive. It is being human, and it too is a perfect way to be. 'Warts and all,' Dad, you are the very best."

26

"Thank you, Julie. Thank you for saying that."

Tears streamed down our faces, as we hugged, kissed, held hands and breathed together, feeling the infinite love and the gift of sharing this time, these words, this joy and peace, this lifetime of father-daughter sharing summed up in a few precious minutes of dialogue.

Laura arrived, along with her daughter LeAndre, who just returned from her wedding trip to Cozumel. Laura hadn't slept well for several days, being with Dad most of the time since Thursday. Her husband Butch and son Nick drove from her nearby hometown to join her and bring her back home. Since I was there, and Dad was looking a little better, Laura thought she'd go home and return to her job for as long as she was able, as long as Dad was holding on okay.

I promised to call if anything changed in his condition, or if I just needed her, and to call her anyway to tell her how it was going. I wouldn't leave her wondering.

That Sunday was a full, full day with Lou, our brother Bob and Marla, his wife, also joining us in the afternoon. We kept Dad busy talking and singing some familiar tunes together. Dad joined us on a few verses.

As we took turns coming, going and just being close with him, he took the opportunity to have his private talk with each one of us, making sure we knew the special quality of his love for us, his assurances and peace with what he was facing, with the prospect of eternity and oneness with God's love.

He asked us each in turn for our agreement with closure, leading us bravely to the very brink of his passing. It exhausted him to have us there for the full day—seventeen of us taking our turns—but he did not complain.

He was surrounded by love.

Late in the afternoon I met my daughter Valerie in the parking lot, as she came to see her granddad. I told her about his condition, improved over the previous two days, and of his private acts of ministry and completion with each of us.

"Be ready," I coached her. She cried and held my hand and bravely faced that prospect.

Soon after we arrived in his room and he acknowledged Val's presence with a smile and a hug, exhaustion overtook Dad. He began to snore loudly as we lingered to visit.

Bob played softly on his guitar several pieces he had written, songs we all loved to hear. Sleeping through this round of singing, I am sure Dad heard it all in his dream state. He so loved Bob's music and each experience of him singing and playing.

Later in the day, Valerie said her goodbyes, Lou flew back to Minnesota, Bob and Marla went home, and I was left with Dad, who barely ate any supper. He scolded himself for not eating better.

"You don't have to eat anything that doesn't taste or feel good right now, Dad. Just eat and drink what you want."

He didn't want.

Soon it was time for him to rest again. The hospice sitter took over at his side as I said goodnight and promised to return in the morning.

I stopped in next door to update Lucy on Dad's condition, and she was glad to know that he rallied somewhat. Starting on the following day, she would be taken in to see him after breakfast. Her doctor granted her permission for one hour of 'sitting up' time in her wheelchair at his bedside. I was so glad to hear this, as I knew this time was precious to them both.

"See you tomorrow, Lucy." I left and walked to my car, feeling more than a little bit otherworldly.

In fact, I had a very hard time focusing on the road and on the driving process—not because I was sad so much as feeling transported.

This was a new world for me, an unexplored aspect of life: the End of Life, being-with dying, communicating the acceptance and completion of my beloved father's time on this plane of existence.

Where am I? Driving on a highway at 65 mph, Julie, so don't forget that.

The tears came after I crawled into bed and spoke with Earl.

Should he come to Tulsa now?

I don't know.

Should he wait? How long?

How can I know for sure?

"Dad seems to have rallied again. Hospice is withdrawing their 24-hour sitters because he was doing so well today. He ate in the morning. He drank. He stayed awake almost the whole day. So, I don't know about timing.

I believe I will appreciate your support more when the time comes, Earl. When he passes. That being said, if you want to see him before then. . ."

Earl elected to wait, not to see him in his last days. He preferred to remember Dad as he was before.

It was so hard to accept the inevitable. I did and I didn't.

Tears helped me gain the equilibrium to fall asleep amidst my swarming thoughts. I reviewed all the day's events, large and small, and braced myself for the next day when I was to be at Dad's bedside for twelve hours.

11

Precious Hours Together

Morning came early. I quickly scanned emails to see if anything couldn't wait and got ready for the day ahead.

I was ready to be with Dad, come what may. And he had a good day.

By the time I arrived, Lucy had come and gone, back to her room and to her bed, minding the doctor's orders: only one hour upright in her wheelchair per day. None of us wanted Lucy to undermine her own healing process.

Dad drifted in and out of a waking and sleeping state, visibly more tired than the previous day.

A few people dropped in. He was ready to say goodbye, quickly.

A few people called, and he preferred not to talk, so I briefly updated them on his condition.

I kept my siblings posted on his status. We emailed, texted and talked on the phone.

Dad was feeling a pressing need to move his bowels and nothing was moving. It was uncomfortable and he brought that to the nurses' attention. They gave him what they could to get things in motion.

At one point, he drew me close and questioned if he had asked me for an agreement around being complete with him.

I assured him that he had and then added, "Daddy, I am here to listen to anything you wish to tell me and anything that is important for you to say now."

He wanted to say it again, to experience his abundant love and blessings pouring out with assurance and appreciation.

We cried, we hugged, we let the time pass in physical contact. I held his hand, he stroked my arm, I rubbed his neck and he leaned forward so I could rub his back a little lower. He sighed with appreciation, "Ahhh. . ."

Daddy, oh, Daddy, "I always loved to rub your back, even as a little girl, and to hear your appreciative sounds."

"Ahhh. . ."

I sang a little, he asked for more, I sang some more. He slept and I read, listening to his breathing, listening to all his little sounds, his coughing, his nose blowing and even his laughter when it came. I asked him what else I could do for him, bring to him—anything that he wanted or needed—a drink, some food, some ChapStick?

He just wanted me to be there, and I was so thankful that I was. These were very precious hours, days or weeks: Who knew? The day passed quickly, much too quickly, all twelve hours. And the sitter took over for the night.

12

Embracing Love Amidst the Pain

Then it was the next day, Tuesday. By my arrival at 10:00AM Lucy had come and gone from his room, and Dad tried to shoo her away even earlier, as his pain and urgency were increasing. He did not want her to scc him in pain.

She told him she would be all right with it; she was his wife and wanted to stay at his side. After an hour, she was taken back to her bed anyway, per the doctor's agreement.

Tuesday was a very different sort of day with Dad than Monday had been. He seemed all right for a while but told me the sensation of needing to move his bowels was periodically very intense now. At the moment he was all right.

His good friend and therapist colleague came by, and Dad rallied for a brief visit despite his preference not to visit with non-family any longer.

"How are you feeling, Armin?"

"Sad and angry and resigned and lots of things. I feel lots of things now," was his response. "Thank you for coming. I'll say goodbye now." He was not interested in sharing more than that with his friend.

"Daddy, would you like to see Kerry?" I asked him about my daughter coming to visit. She had just texted me with that query and to ask about his condition. "She could come and have lunch here and sit with you while she studies for awhile. Would you like that?"

"Yes, I would like to see Kerry. Yes, that would be very good."

And so, I called her, saying, "Granddaddy is 'up and down,' and sometimes he's in a lot of discomfort. When I asked him about seeing you, he said that to visit with you would be very good. Please do come, Kerry."

When Kerry arrived, she brightened his smile with her greeting and they hugged. He asked about her university classes and about how everything else was going with her. She shared some details about school and her part-time jobs: teaching Hebrew to other young Jewish children, dog walking and grading math and physics tests for university professors.

"Wow, Kerry, that sounds like a full and wonderful schedule!" her granddad said with enthusiasm.

She settled in to hold his hand while sitting and chatting. Later, Kerry privately remarked to me that in this moment she realized it was the first time she'd held her grandfather's hands as an adult. She noticed how soft and strong and wonderful his hands felt in hers. Being able to reflect on those moments of this awareness was a very special event for her.

34

For a good long while, we sat with Kerry on one side of Dad's bed and me on the other, both holding his hands.

Then he tugged on Kerry's arm. He tugged harder till he firmly pulled her up from her seat and close to him on the bed. There he held her in a gentle embrace. She laid her head across his chest, and as Dad patted her hair, he gave her his eternal assurances of love and hope and life. He told her she was his one and only Kerry, a special granddaughter and a special person whom he loves, and God loves, always. "It matters not what name you call God. He always hears and always listens, and is always there for you, Kerry. God is love."

Kerry looked up into my eyes as he softly spoke to her, with tears streaming down her face, holding my hand in her left and his hand in her right, and saying, "Yes, Granddaddy," while receiving all his loving affirmations.

Then he asked her, "What is the name for God, the Hebrew name that Jesus might have used when calling out to God from the cross?"

Through her tears Kerry answered him, "Adonai, Granddaddy, the name is *Adonai*."

And he repeated, "Adonai, Adonai."

Then he looked at me and said, "Julie, will you remind me of that later? If I cannot remember, will you remind me of the name *Adonai*?"

"Yes, of course, Daddy. I will remind you."

And he repeated, again, "Adonai, Adonai."

Kerry wept and smiled through her tears, as she realized the gift she had just given to him. On her face, the joy and the sadness were equally evident. And she stayed in his embrace until he was done giving her his special blessing.

I had witnessed this now several times, his ministry to us sons and daughters and grandchildren. Each time it was done in an individualized way with each of us left feeling such a loving bond and knowing that a special moment had just been shared. I was in awe of my father's presence of mind and heart to be able to give us such a treasure in words and loving kindness in his last days. Later I learned he had done the same for my stepsiblings too. The man had so much giving in him, right up until the end. I have no doubts that he and Lucy shared their own precious words as they completed their time together.

Soon after she ate lunch, Kerry nodded off in Dad's recliner, wrapped in his prayer shawl with her school-books open on her lap. She awoke and left in short order to complete her schoolwork. The nap wasn't planned; it was her way of equilibrating after a strong emotional exchange. She didn't regret the time, but now she had to go. Dad thanked Kerry for being with him and said goodbye.

As the day went on, I witnessed his pain level increase exponentially, and there was little the nurses could do to ease it. They gave him what medicine they had available per doctors' orders, and we finally called for something stronger.

It was time for a new strategy. Was he impacted? What was happening inside causing him so much pressure? When the nurse finally came to check him, she concluded there was not much that could be done to physically relieve him. The pain was due to increasing tumor mass in his abdomen; that was the best assessment without the use of hospital technologies, and Dad was all done with those.

Being at his side, hearing his groans and cries, was—I can only imagine—like attending an unsuccessful birth, with the agony building and building and his energy waning. Incessant waves of pain were wearing him out. He did not wish to drink or eat. He wanted relief, and he asked God to bring it to him. Each time it lessened, he said his thanks out loud.

I asked what I could do and he assured me there was nothing else; my being there was enough. He was sorry I had to see him and hear him like this.

I was concerned that Lucy next door was listening to his anguished cries and would worry. I checked in with her briefly while the nurses checked Dad's condition. Lucy had heard his cries, but until I told her what the source was, she assumed they were coming from another room, not Dad's.

Oops.

I didn't want to leave him in such a state, and I was glad that during the last hours of the evening his pain eased considerably. His relative comfort made me feel better about going to my own bed to rest when the night sitter arrived to look after Dad. I said my goodbyes, though he was already dozing, and told the sitter I would return by 10:00AM.

And that was my intention.

After driving home and calling Earl for some reassuring words of comfort, I finally crawled between the sheets and let my own exhaustion take over.

13

Self-Care

On Wednesday I awoke with an obvious upper respiratory infection and knew right away that I couldn't be at Dad's side. I was feeling sicker by the minute. With less than three hours till my 'shift' started, I had to act quickly. I called Laura and she promptly called the in-home nursing agency to enlist a day sitter for his bedside needs.

Then I called Dad to let him know, and the attending nurse aide helped to convey to him my dilemma. He said to just take care of me, and he understood. He said he felt better, again eating something that morning. His report reassured me. I started a self-care routine of hot tea and lemon, vinegar and honey, Vitamin C and rest. I felt pretty awful, physically and emotionally, and beat myself up about not being there for Dad. I slept, woke, drank and slept some more.

My brother Bob came from Tahlequah for a visit with Dad that evening, and I was so glad that he could make it. He stayed much longer than he intended, perhaps sensing that it might be his last opportunity.

Dad did better all that day, while I got worse, feeling wiped out and sleeping most of the day and night.

14

What to Do?

I felt no better on Thursday. I had let my father and my family down, or so I felt. I focused on getting better.

Laura drove to Tulsa to be with Dad by mid-afternoon on Thursday. She said he didn't look much worse than when she left on Sunday, but he increasingly complained about pain again.

Laura and Lou and the hospice nurse had an evening phone rendezvous about what to do next, as Dad's current medications were not strong enough to ease this level of pain. We all knew that adding morphine would hasten the shutdown of bodily functions; he had problems with those side effects after past operations. Everyone was prepared to give him morphine when the time was right. We didn't want him to suffer and Dad didn't want to suffer either.

15

Time to Ease the Pain

On Friday, I came to visit him from across the room. I sucked on cough lozenges and kept him company while Laura took a short break. As soon as she returned, I went home again to rest after promising to be back the next day; that was the best I could do. Surely I would feel better by Saturday.

Dad's comfort level worsened significantly after I left, and Laura had an afternoon with him much like I had experienced on Tuesday, with increasing intensity and frequency of pain in returning cycles.

All agreed it was time for the morphine. Soon after it was administered, thankfully, his pained eased.

16

Being-with My Dad at the End of Life

Saturday morning, I awoke feeling marginally better, still coughing and fairly exhausted. I touched base with Laura and then got ready to join her.

This was also prom day for my daughter Valerie. She had a full day of plans with friends leading up to the big dance. We chatted about the upcoming fun while we both ate breakfast.

After taking a shower and sipping on one last hot drink, I was ready to go and be with Dad. I felt sure I needed to get there *now*.

When I arrived, Laura and her daughter LeAndre were both at Dad's side. He was groggy but aware that we were there, and we talked so he could hear what we were saying. Laura told me that the morphine eased his pain. He seemed to be resting peacefully and was barely responsive to us.

Laura and LeAndre went to purchase some ointment to apply to his drying eyes that now stayed partly open all the time. The two of them were ready for a short break, and I was ready to be present.

These were precious end-of-life moments; that was very obvious from Dad's appearance. His fingers and toes were starting to swell and darken slightly as his circulation waned.

I took his hand in mine, talked to him and rubbed his arm, his neck and his smooth head. I kissed his cheek and reminded him that I loved him. Though not able to speak clearly, he acknowledged my presence with some sounds.

Soon I noticed that his hands had darkened even more, and when I checked them, I found that his feet had also. The nurse aide came and checked on us and also noted the purple color. She said that meant his passing might be quite soon.

When she left the room, I decided to try my voice, despite its cold-induced roughness, and sing *The Lord's Prayer*. Dad had requested that song on Tuesday and my singing was disappointing to me then. I hoped I could do a better job singing to him now—and I did, despite some inevitable tears in the middle.

Then I was breathing, breathing and being-with, being right there at his side.

I envisioned my grandmother Carrie and grandfather Armin in the room with us, reaching out to Dad and softly calling his name. While feeling their presence so strongly, I said to him, "I love you, Daddy. We all love you—Lucy, Laura, Louis and Bob, and each member of our family—and we are ready for you to release your struggle to live. We are ready for you to go when you are ready to go. I love you so much and I know that your love will endure, just as you told me. It will be with me always and with each of us."

He made soft sounds in response, no clear words, but he acknowledged me.

"Daddy, your mother Carrie and father Armin are waiting with open arms to welcome you home. When you are ready, they are right here to greet you."

I reminded him, as he previously asked me to do, of the Hebrew name for God, saying, "Daddy, Adonai is here right now and is ready to receive your spirit. Adonai is ready to welcome you home."

With great effort, Dad mouthed, "Adonai, Adonai."

I held him and waited.

I listened and watched.

I felt his abundant love and peace in the moment.

I cried.

With the name of God on his lips, Dad took his last breath. As the seconds ticked by, I realized this was so. Adonai heard him and answered his prayer for release— immediately, peacefully and gently.

This is it.

I glanced at the clock to note the time of his transition. Wrapping my arms around his shoulders, I repeated my assurances of love and life. I looked up to greet the angels that most assuredly filled the room. I looked up to see Daddy taking flight, freed from the burdens of old age and failing health, free to fly. I looked up and let the tears flow.

I will miss you so much, Daddy. I will miss your eyes and your smile, your soft skin, your warm heart, your words, your silliness, your guidance, your memories, your laughter, your wisdom, your experience, your loving kindness. . . Oh, Daddy, I will miss all of you so very much. Always.

17

At Peace

Several minutes passed, and a nurse aide appeared. From the doorway she immediately guessed and said gently, "Oh, is it that time?"

"Yes, it's over. He has passed."

"Do you know the exact time?"

I told her the minute I believed he took his last breath. She asked me if I was all right, double-checked Dad's absence of a pulse, then went to call for someone to officially pronounce his passing.

I called Laura, who was just in the store parking lot heading back to be with us. It had only been a few minutes since she and LeAndre left Dad's room. And only a few before that when I arrived.

I went next door to tell Lucy, who accepted the news well. It was expected and his release from the pain and struggle was a relief. Now he was at rest and at peace.

My phone rang. It was my niece Monica calling from Seattle to talk to her grandfather. I tried to comfort her while I conveyed the sad news. She was very upset. I told her I was preparing to telephone Lou—her dad—and I suggested she call him soon after I did.

"I'm too late to talk to Granddaddy, and I left too soon when I saw him for the last time," she said through her tears. I assured Monica that she had given her grandfather a very precious gift of cuddle time when she visited—embracing him as only she could do, curled up in his bed at his side.

Before I concluded my call with Monica, both my daughters Kerry and Valerie placed calls to my cell phone. They happened to be together when they heard the sad news and were glad to comfort each other in that moment.

Valerie was getting ready for her prom date and I wished her a happy evening, assuring her that her granddad would have wanted her to enjoy that time. "We knew this time was coming, Val, and we'll be grieving tomorrow and the next day. Please enjoy your time with friends, and call me if you want to talk at any point in the evening," I told her.

Kerry and I briefly discussed her granddad's final moments. Later, I sent her the following text message: "Granddaddy took his last breath at 4:22, mouthing the word 'Adonai.' You gave him that name for God and it was on his lips as he went home to rest." Somehow she knew that would be his last word.

Then I called my brother Lou. He was not surprised, but his sorrow was audible. I wished he had been present to see how peacefully Dad took this last earthly step. I told him to expect a call from Monica soon after we hung up.

Bob was next to hear the news, and he comforted me as I conveyed my mixture of sadness and relief in the experience of Dad's last moments. His voice and his words soothed me.

When I called Earl in Toronto his grief was also audible. He would be with me soon and that gladdened me. I was missing him too after a week apart.

In short order, Lou sent an email with a poem attached, explaining to each of us family recipients that he was composing it in the very moments of Dad's passing. *Farewell, Dear Father* lives on as a heart-felt poetic tribute to our dad, and I am so thankful that Lou shared it with us all. I responded to Lou's email by sending out a brief account of my last moments with Dad, so that all our family members might know the peaceful manner in which he passed.

The nurse aides brought my stepmom Lucy to be at Dad's side. Laura and LeAndre also returned.

We waited with Dad until his body was transported out of the building. It was a major shift, to be complete with his passing. The process of moving on had begun.

18

A Celebration of Life and a Legacy of Love

My father requested that after his passing we hold a Celebration of Life and, in the manner of Friends (Quakers), invite those in attendance to 'share from the heart' as they may feel ready. We held this event nearly two weeks after his death.

Many who personally knew and loved my dad, or who were there to support our family, attended—a much greater number than we anticipated. As more and more people arrived, chairs were added to the many already placed in the large meeting room of the retirement facility where he and Lucy happily resided for the last several years. Dad enjoyed a rich life of daily community and camaraderie with the other retired residents, and a great number came to celebrate his life with us.

Family members, some who lived close by and others who came a great distance, participated in the gathering. Also attending were his and Lucy's personal friends; colleagues from various stages of Dad's work experiences; members of his writers group; Quakers from our local, and other nearby, Meetings for Worship and so on.

Our bereaving family was supported by the presence of our own friends, many of whom hadn't known Dad personally. I was grateful to the many who made this memorial time a priority, taking time off work to attend, support and create a memorable tribute to a beloved man.

The vocal sharing of personal testimonials, poetry and song by so many of the various attendees on that day created newly inspiring and enriching memories, the legacy of Dad's love and his devoted life's work enduring in each of the lives he touched. Story after story touched our hearts and illustrated the wide scope of his impact as a Civil Rights advocate, social worker, therapist, colleague, relative, friend, life partner, father, stepfather, grandfather and great-grandfather.

Had he been alive and physically present at this event, Dad would have hesitated to take credit and accept the abundance of appreciative accolades. I feel quite certain that he *was* indeed present and, knowing each heart and mind from his 'spirited' perspective, able to truly comprehend the legacy of his love and the depth of his impact on so many lives.

Accept it, Daddy. You left your mark on us all.

19

A Wonderful End of Life

Now I know from experience there is such a thing as a wonderful End of Life, one that nurtures both the dying and the bereaved. My dying dad ministered to his family, leaving each of us with special memories—even of his last moments with us.

He passed while I held his hand, talked and sang to him. I'm so grateful that I was present and that I got to say to him, "You will always be with me, and I with you. My heart and your heart are one. Thank you for your endless love. Thank you for being the very best dad I could ever have."

I picked up the pen where you left off, Daddy. Grieving your loss is a long, long road—just barely traveled. Memories of you keep me company when I miss you, which I do every day. I take the little spurts of sorrow as they come and give thanks for the closeness that makes your passing so hard to accept sometimes.

I know that you know: I love you.

20

Lightbody Reunion: My Astral Travel Experience

Three or four days after my father passed, I had a vivid dream. Taking the form of my 'lightbody,' I went along with my father's on an astral journey, playing and romping throughout the galaxies. We merged, separated, went anywhere and everywhere, experienced being anything and everything as well as nothing. We paused, indefinitely, and then zoomed from place to place at light speed.

It was a never-ending experience in each boundless moment, our being-ness immeasurable in place and time. We were Light Essence. Soul. Source.

Eventually, the sheer intensity of the joy that I felt brought me fully awake. My sleeping physical self could no longer contain that immense level of feeling.

For hours I lay awake and processed what I had seen and experienced. Even in the immediate moments after the dream, I already felt its clarity slipping from my conscious grasp. I saw things that words cannot adequately describe and am saddened that as time passed I lost the vividness and the experiential 'glory'—there's a good word for it.

It was a journey of such depth and wonder and far beyond the capacity of the human mind—my finite mind—to create such an experience. I believe it was a Soul Dance of the highest order.

I am so grateful to have had that time with my dad. As I mentioned earlier, we had a brief lightbody union shortly before he passed, a sampling of the future dream trip we would share.

There are some 'dangers' inherent in such vivid transcendent experiences. I had lots of desire to be in that lightbody state exclusively over the following few weeks. With such a strong Remembrance of Soul it was often hard to be 'right here, right now.' Even so, I am well anchored to my physical being. I love my pleasures, tolerate my pains and have no premature death wish. I cherish my earthly connections to humans and joyously celebrate every heartstring.

As the weeks and months pass, I find pleasure and value in returning to the rapturous feeling and joyful memory of our interstellar dream journey. Those moments refresh; raise my consciousness and awareness; and infuse me with peace, healing and joy.

Writing about Dad's last weeks of life is also helpful to my grieving heart. With each phase of writing, rewriting, editing and reading, I cry a bit less and celebrate a bit more.

The Life of Armin Louis Saeger, Jr., aka *Daddy*, is a great cause for celebration. His End of Life was beautiful, memorable and as special as he was.

My grandfather Armin, Sr., once said to my dad in another context, "It's all part of life, Armin. It's all part of life." And so it is with the part of life called death.

The End.

This is it.

Julie Saeger Nierenberg
October 2, 2012

21

A Life Well Lived, a Man Well Loved

Armin Louis Saeger, Jr., 87, died Saturday, April 28, 2012, in Tulsa, OK. He was born in Philadelphia, PA, on April 11, 1925, to Caroline Roeger and Armin Saeger.

In keeping with his Quaker beliefs, Armin served his country in Alternate Service, including human guinea pig experiments during WWII, and he was active in the early Civil Rights Movement. After graduating from Earlham College, Armin and his wife Mary Jane became Mission Directors at Kickapoo Friends Center in McCloud, OK. He earned his Masters of Social Work at The University of Oklahoma, and became a social worker at US Public Health Service Indian Hospital in Tahlequah. In 1966, he began work at the national level as Executive Director of the Indian Rights Association. He then took a clinical position at the Tulsa Psychiatric Center and became an Accredited Bioenergetic Therapist. Eventually, Armin practiced privately.

He enjoyed gardening in his extensively landscaped yard, often a featured stop on The Tulsa Water Garden Tour. During Armin's retirement years at Inverness Village, he was active in a local writers group and published a collection of insightful, heartwarming memoirs, *Sowing My Quaker Oats*, to the delight of his family and friends. His peaceful essence and varied accomplishments touched others in meaningful and lasting ways. Armin leaves behind his wife Lucy of 35 years, four children, three stepchildren, a loving extended family, and a host of friends.

22

Sowing a Seed

Each of us can be prepared to be-with others at the end of life. Most of us will be within that scenario in one role or another at some point in our lives. Preparing ourselves for these inevitable circumstances will bring added peace and presence to our daily lives right now.

I hope this little book about my own family's journey through our father's end of life contributes a story that touches your heart while it informs you of resources and options. Its creation was motivated by my belief in the possibility of a beautiful, peaceful and fulfilling death, as informed by my own experience with my dad.

I leave it with you now, as a seed of the legacy my dad planted here on earth. I believe, just as he told me, that love is eternally with us.

23

Gratitude

Members of our family leaned on each other for mutual support through Dad's last few years of life. We do so now as we continue to mourn his loss and celebrate his life. I am thankful for each one's special contribution to our family circle.

As my father lived with cancer and its side effects, many special friends performed acts of kindness by visiting; sending cards, music and letters; offering rides, meals, and grocery shopping excursions—just to name a few. One friend stepped up repeatedly to stay with my dad in the hospital when we could not be there. We have so much gratitude for every act of support that was shown and offered to our family.

In his last months of life, Dad was honored with speaking invitations, and he was awarded an acknowledgment for his spirited resolve to live fully and energetically among his peers. These were moments to treasure, and he sure did. I'm so glad he got to experience them.

Those who worked with my father in the months, weeks and days leading up to the end of his life did a wonderful job taking care of his medical needs. They also did their best taking care of his nonmedical needs, supporting us while caring for him. I feel compassion for the doctors who conveyed my dad's end-of-life information to him and to me as his companion in the hospital. We can all get better at this process.

I am most grateful for my father's skillful guidance through his own transition. His training as a social worker and therapist, his emotional honesty and his ministry to those around him assisted us all to face the inevitable end.

24

How Can You Create Peace of Mind?

From my dad's and my family's living example, I suggest that you consider taking these steps, both for your own experience of peace and for that of your loved ones:

- Acknowledge the important people in your life and give credit for their role.

- Leave a legacy—your story—for all who come after to treasure.

- Ask if all is okay between you and each of your loved ones. If not, make it so.

- Forgive generously and ask forgiveness. Unburden your heart.

- Give thanks to each person for whom you are thankful.

- Show your love in every way possible.

- Ask and answer any questions that remain—about final wishes, end-of-life medical care and the unsolved mysteries in your lives.

- Express your beliefs, fears and assurances. Welcome those held by others.

- Accept and embrace All That Is, giving thanks for Life.

- Say "goodbye" or "so long."

Why wait till the End of Life to take these actions? They will change the quality of the rest of your life immeasurably if you decide to take them sooner than later.

25

Resources: Getting the Support You Need

Peace is a much harder thing to find in one's heart and mind when there are any doubts how someone's care is handled, especially when suspicion that something was overtly wrong is grounded in obvious clues. This lack of peace is common to many bereaved families who are not adequately supported or counseled about options, causation and probable outcomes.

Too many times, a person's life is impacted by unfulfilling, terrifying or guilt-ridden experiences of the death of a family member. Some live with great doubts and gripping fears as a result of their inability to be at peace with what transpires. These feelings may not arise from experiences of overt catastrophe or violence, but rather they result from the heart trauma of being forced to choose life or death on behalf of another. Far too many are left without support at these critical times, misunderstanding or misinterpreting events and questioning where they themselves may be in the future—scared, confused, unsupported, unable to communicate, in pain, etc.

Some feel this fright so intimately that the concept of dying consequently stunts their living. I feel great sadness about this situation and also great motivation to connect others to healing support and vital education about being-with dying. Following are two insightful resources provided by experts dedicated to making the end-of-life experience a better one.

Virginia Seno, PhD
The Esse Institute
www.esseinstitute.com

Earlier in the same spring of my father's death, I was privileged to meet a nurse educator whose specialty is training clinicians, clergy, hospice support teams and others how to communicate with and be-with the dying and the bereaved. Reading her blog posts and other online resources gave me new insight into the lack of skills that many professionals have in this vital area of caregiving and support. I strongly recommend Virginia Seno, PhD, and the Esse Institute that she established to provide training and support to those who work professionally, or as volunteers, with the dying and their loved ones. I encourage you to take advantage of the many web-accessible resources that Dr. Seno offers through the Esse Institute. She provides a downloadable 4-Lesson Mini-Course that will benefit anyone who invests the few hours it takes to complete.

Dr. Monica Williams-Murphy and Kris Murphy
It's OK to Die™
http://oktodie.com

The Murphys have established an online presence to educate and assist us all to "make peace with life" and to plan in advance for the creation of a peaceful and transforming death. They empower their readers with a variety of tools, checklists and resources; and they provide a venue to share stories and concerns—all with the ultimate goal of preparing us for this inevitable and powerful time: the End of Life.

70

26

Write Your Story
Leave a Legacy for Your Loved Ones

In my father's last decade, he wrote a series of memoirs that he then self-published. It was a labor of love for a man whose eyesight was increasingly compromised year after year. Focusing on the writing process stirred his memory of happy childhood events, times with family and boyhood friends, teenaged milestones, character-shaping life decisions, surprising twists and adventurous turns of his social work career, significant family events, unique historical insights, etc. These short glimpses of my dad's perspective on life, captured in simple stories, eventually became the chapters of his book *Sowing My Quaker Oats*.

Are you interested in creating a book that captures your stories in your words, for your family – and others – to read and savor?

I encourage you to begin now! If you type, you can record your own words and save them digitally to your computer. If not, you can record them on a voice recorder and later transcribe them. There are even computer programs that perform such tasks. Saving your voice recording for your loved ones to listen to is also a great idea.

Writing can be as easy as talking, especially when you know that you have someone to help you edit the final product to be print-ready.

Would you benefit from a writing coach to help you begin your story and be accountable to reach your goals?

Would you like an editor to give you feedback and constructive criticism along the way?

If you would like me to assist you to leave your own written legacy, here's how you may contact me:

info@createwriteenterprises.com

Julie Saeger Nierenberg
CreateWrite Enterprises
www.createwriteenterprises.com

Made in the USA
Charleston, SC
09 January 2014